# The Christmas Book

## Jane Bull

DK PUBLISHING

LONDON, NEW YORK, MUNICH,
MELBOURNE AND DELHI

DESIGN • Jane Bull
TEXT • Penelope York
PHOTOGRAPHY • Andy Crawford
DESIGN ASSISTANCE • Claire Penny

MANAGING ART EDITOR • Rachael Foster
PUBLISHING MANAGER • Mary Ling
DTP DESIGNER • Almudena Díaz

For Charlotte, Billy,
and James

First American Edition, 2001

03 04 05 10 9 8 7 6 5 4 3 2

Published in the United States by
DK Publishing, Inc.
375 Hudson Street
New York, NY 10014

DK Publishing offers special discounts for bulk purchases for sales promotions or
premiums. Specific, large-quantity needs can be met with special editions, including
personalized covers, excerpts of existing guides, and corporate imprints. For more
information, contact Special Services Markets Department, DK Publishing, Inc.,
375 Hudson Street, New York, NY 10014 Tel: 212-213-4800

Library of Congress Cataloging-in-Publication Data

Bull, Jane. 1957-
        The Christmas book/Jane Bull.--1st American ed.
            p.cm
        ISBN 0-7894-7873-0
        1. Christmas--Juveline leterature. 2. Christmas decorations--
Juvenile literature. [1.Christmas decorations. 2. Handicraft.] I. Title.

GT4985.5 .B85 2001
394.2663--dc21

2001017394

ISBN: 0-7894-7873-0

Color reproduction by GRB Editrice S.r.l., Verona, Italy
Printed and bound in Italy by L.E.G.O.

Discover more at
**www.dk.com**

# Christmas is coming . . .

## Christmas Countdown

Christmas Countdown 4-5

How to make your Advent Box 6-7

Greetings from the 3rd Dimension 8-9

How to make 3-D Greeting Cards 10-11

## Deck the Halls

Paper Snow 12-13

Baubles, Orbs, and Pompoms 14-15

How to make Pompoms and Baubles 16-17

Christmas Tree 18-19

How to make Tree Decorations 20-21

Merry Mobiles 22-23 * Storm in a Jelly Jar 24-25

How to make a Swirling Snowstorm 26-27

Santa's on the Move 28-29

A Winter Wonderland 30-31

How to make Gift Boxes 32-33

## A Feast of Pleasures

Host of Angels 34-35

Santa's Cookie Factory 36-37

Frosty Welcomes 38-39

How does your Garden Glow? 40-41

Pass the Present 42-43

That's Entertainment! 44-45

Packing Presents 46-47

Index 48

Christmas starts here

Open up No1 and begin your countdown

# Christmas Countdown

## The buildup to Christmas will never be the same again with this 3-D, advent box-calendar. It'll help the days fly by!

Discover the delights in every drawer

4

No more boxes left to open? It must be Christmas!

# HOW TO MAKE YOUR ADVENT BOX

All you need for this spectacular advent box-calendar is one large cereal box and 23 little boxes. On the first of December open the main doors, then each day until Christmas eve open a box to reveal a surprise.

Ask an adult . .
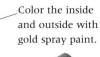
for help with the spraying

Cut down the center of a cereal box to create doors.

Cut out another piece of cardboard for the decorative top.

Color the inside and outside with gold spray paint.

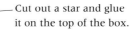

Cut out a star and glue it on the top of the box.

Stick flat boxes on the inside of the doors. Check that the calendar can shut properly.

Glue the boxes in place – you can create any Christmas shape you like with them.

Decorate the calendar with torn pieces of foil and glue a star on each little box to write the numbers on.

CANDY WRAPPER    TORN FOIL    STICKERS    TREE SHAPES    CRAFT GLUE

# Collect 23 little boxes to put inside

Try out different arrangements with the boxes.

Paint the boxes with acrylic paint and craft glue mixed together.

Cut doors in the boxes and use paper fasteners as handles.

Drape tinsel around the box for an extra sparkle, and decorate the star.

Tie on a cardboard star with the number '1' on it.

# Open one box a day 'til Christmas!

Fill the boxes with goodies – candy, jokes, messages, or toys.

Glue down small, plastic bottle caps for handles.

Tie a bow onto the doors to keep them shut.

Write the numbers on each box inside from 2-24.

Create a card with piles and piles of presents

Christmas Greetings

# Greetings
## From the 3rd Dimension

Bouncing Rudolphs, sticking-out snowmen,
leaping stars, and a Santa bearing a bouncing gift.

They're out of this World!

# HOW TO MAKE 3-D GREETING CARDS

Make sure your card is the first to be noticed on the mantlepiece with these pop-up, springing, bobbing, greeting cards!

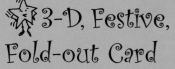

Open it up and out it pops

## ★ Template

These templates are for the Christmas tree, the snowman, and the presents. Cut the solid lines and fold the dotted lines. Trace them onto your folded construction paper.

Be careful not to draw your picture over half-way across the card or the fold will stick out too much when the card is closed.

FOLD CARD HERE

## ★ 3-D, Festive, Fold-out Card

From a flat card to a pile of presents in a Christmas flash! Four simple cuts and your greeting cards are transformed. Try the snowman and Christmas tree designs, too.

10

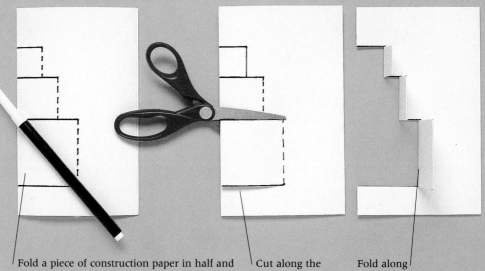

Fold a piece of construction paper in half and draw on the presents template, as shown.

Cut along the solid lines.

Fold along the dotted lines.

# ✦ Pop-up Wobble Card

With this magic spring card, you can make anything appear to jump out at the person who receives it – from Rudolph's nose to Santa's present or a twinkling star. Try out some of your own designs. How about some springing, jangling bells, or a snowman spring?

Rudolph's nose

Cut out a piece of construction paper and fold it in half.

Cut Rudolf's face and nose out of two other colors of paper. Glue the face onto the main card.

## Help Rudolph's nose wibble and wobble!

Draw a swirl on a piece of construction paper – no bigger than Rudolph's nose – and cut it out.

Glue the center of the spring to the back of the nose.

Glue the other end of the spring to Rudolph's face.

Complete Rudolph by drawing on his features.

Cut out some construction paper, slightly bigger than the original cut-out one.

Glue the construction paper to the backing piece, matching the folds in the middle.

Decorate the card with stickers or colored foil.

# Paper Snow

## A flurry of paper snowflakes

float and swirl through the sky, settling in the branches of the trees.

Take a piece of paper and fold it in half twice along the dotted lines.

Your paper will look like this.

Fold it in half again.

*Snowstorms of snowflakes!*

Hang up your snowflake with thread.

Now snip away, then unfold the flake.

See what shapes unfold

Get wrapped up in these paper pompoms

Baubles, Orbs, and Pompoms

Scrodtiss

Baubles to hang on trees or orbs to hang from ceilings.

14

Transform flat cards into shapely spheres

## ✦ Hanging Around

Glittering baubles and giant orbs swinging
and spinning around your room give it a
magical Christmassy feel. All you need are old comic strips,
wrapping paper, greeting cards, postcards, or anything else
that's bright – just make sure you are allowed to cut it up!

15

# HOW TO MAKE POMPOMS AND BAUBLES

## Paper Pompoms

Pompoms can be made out of any paper you like. Christmas wrapping paper is jolly and bright, or you could decorate your own paper with a Christmas pattern using paint or stickers.

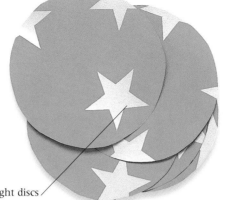

Cut out eight discs of paper (about template size below).

Fold the bunch of discs in half and staple down the crease.

## Baubles and Orbs

Festive baubles can be hung on trees or simply left to spin from ceilings. When you have mastered the bauble, try making the spectacular, giant orb with 20 decorated paper plates. You'll have your work cut out finding room for something that big!

Take a stack of old Christmas cards and trace around the template.

Cut out 20 circles, and snip out the notches – see template.

*Use this template to cut out 20 discs*

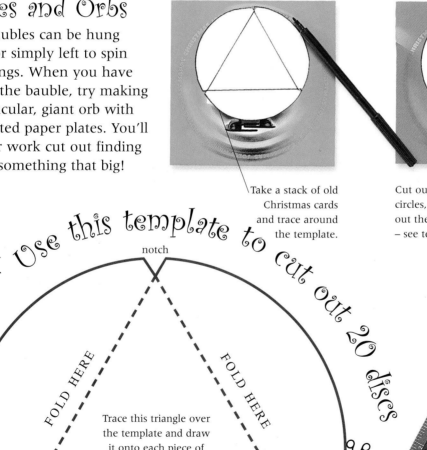

notch

FOLD HERE

FOLD HERE

Trace this triangle over the template and draw it onto each piece of construction paper.

notch

FOLD HERE

notch

To help you fold, run a blunt-ended pen down the dotted lines.

16

Tape a piece of string down the middle.

Take one layer from each side and staple them together at the bottom.

Pick up a new layer from the left side and staple it to the left top flap.

Continue stapling the layers alternately from top to bottom until it is finished.

Staple the flaps together at each end. Keep stapling them together until they become an orb shape.

To hang up your bauble, make a hole and tie some string through it.

Make a giant orb using 20 paper plates.

Wow! it's almost as big as me!

# Decorate your tree with glittering goodies

## Turn me into a dangling tree ornament

## Tree Art

There's nothing better than a tree weighed down by colorful decorations to remind you that it's Christmas. Even better if you have made them all yourself.

## Deck the Tree

Table-tennis-ball angel heads, dangling Santas, glittering baubles, yogurt cup goody baskets, a foil star – they look amazing and are simple to make, too.

# Christmas Tree

Turn your bedroom into a festive delight by trimming a tree with an explosion of colorful ornaments.

# How to Make Tree Ornaments

## Salt Dough Dangles

10¹/₂ oz (300 g) plain flour
10¹/₂ oz (300 g) salt
7 fl oz (200 ml) water
1 teaspoon oil

Put all of the ingredients into a bowl and dig in.

Squeeze it together to make a ball of dough.

Cook for 20 minutes
350°F (180°C)
Cool on a wire rack before painting.

Cut out shapes with a cookie cutter or a knife.

Make a base and pinch off pieces of dough to make features.

Don't forget to make a hole in them with a toothpick before you cook them, so that you can hang them up.

*Ask an adult . . .*
to help with the oven

Delicious as they look, these decorations aren't very tasty!

*Ho, ho, ho!*

Remember the hole.

Add some string.

20   Make Santa's dough head    Build his face    Heat him up    Color him in

# Glitter Card Dangles

All you need for these sparkling dangles is some cardboard and lots of decorations – go wild with the sequins!

Draw some shapes on a piece of cardboard.

Cut the shapes out.

Glue on some colored foil and sequins.

Make a hole in the top with a toothpick.

Thread some string through the hole.

Add more and more sequins!

# Angel Head

Transform a cheap table-tennis ball into a beautiful angel's face in seconds.

Make a hole at the top and bottom.

Thread string through and knot at the bottom.

Wind string around your fingers.

Tie it in the middle.

Cut the edges.

Glue the hair to the head.

Decorate the face.

# Candy Cups

Fill this doll-sized basket, made out of a yogurt cup, with tasty treats.

Cut off the rim.

Glue on a ribbon handle.

Decorate and fill with candies. Yum yum!

# Tree Top

A cardboard star smothered in glittery candy wrappers finishes off your tree perfectly. Dress up your tree and make sure no one steals the candy!

Shredded foil candy wrappers.

Glue pieces of foil onto the cardboard star.

To hang it on the tree, attach a band of construction paper to the back with glue.

Decorate your tree with lots of glitzy colors!

# Merry Mobiles

## Christmas is on the move.

Hang Rudolphs, Santas, wintry snowmen, and tree faces around your room and you'll be spinning!

*Cut out shapes from cardboard and jazz them up*

Use cardboard for your mobiles.

Glitter will catch the light when the mobiles spin and give the room an extra sparkle.

*Paint the eyes*

These ornaments make great tree eyes.

Table-tennis ball eyes.

*Give the nose an extra sparkle*

Make a hole at the top and bottom, thread some string through, and knot.

Feeling dizzy yet?

It's meltdown for the snowman!

### In a Spin

Hang these fantastic mobiles from the ceiling and watch them spinning and twirling around. Remember to paint and decorate them on both sides so that whichever way they turn you can see exactly what they are.

# Storm
# in a Jelly Jar

## Shake up the snow!

Catch some Christmas magic and keep it in a jar.

Wow! These **sparkle** more than me!

This penguin feels right at home!

Exploding star burst!

# HOW TO MAKE A SWIRLING SNOWSTORM

For your stormy winter wonderlands, all you need are some screw-top jars, water, glycerine, glitter, and a few toys. Add them together, and you have a perfect gift for all the movers and shakers you know!

shake, whirl, and SWIRL!!

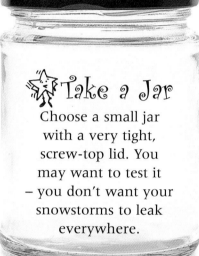

## ⭐ Take a Jar

Choose a small jar with a very tight, screw-top lid. You may want to test it – you don't want your snowstorms to leak everywhere.

**1** Add glitter to glycerine

**2** Fill up with water

**3** Give it a stir

WATER

GLYCERINE

PLASTIC TOY

STRONG GLUE

GLITTER

## Glycerine

Glycerine is a nontoxic liquid that can be bought in most pharmacies. It slightly thickens the water so that your glitter snow falls more slowly when you shake it. Use about one part glycerine to two parts water.

## Glue Tip

Use a strong glue that seals even when in water to attach the toy. For an extra seal, add some glue around the lid, as well as inside the rim, to prevent leakage.

no great shakes
they're easy
to make

Glue around the inside of the lid and the outside of the jar rim.

Decorate the lid with festive ribbon.

4 — Stick down a toy

5 — Screw the lid on tightly

6 — Shake it up!

# Santa's on the Move

## Jingle bells! Santa's on his way. Give him a little time to fill his sleigh with goodies and he'll be up in the sky in a flash.

### ✦ Candy Factory

All it takes to create Santa's chalet and sleigh are lots of goodies and lots of imagination. When you have built your sleigh, fill it up with bundles of bright candies and cookies – don't be tempted to eat them – and display them on the Christmas table.

# Sugar snow sprinkled

through a paper doily provides a snowy landscape for the reindeer to visit

# HOW TO BUILD SANTA'S CHALET AND SLEIGH

All you need is a piece of cardboard as the sleigh base and a milk carton for the chalet.

Cookie layer glued down.

Cardboard base.

## Sugary Glue

Mix confectionary sugar and water to make a sticky paste. Spread it on with a knife and press your cookies down on top of it.

Chocolate mini-rolls and fingers.

Bars of chocolate.

Cut off the bottom of the carton if it is too tall.

Paste on chocolate fingers as logs for the house.

A cracker makes a good front to start building on.

## Candy canes for speedy runners

Remember to leave enough room on the base for the runners.

A cookie for Santa to rest his back on.

## Sticky Tip

If your roof keeps slipping down, put the box into the fridge for a few minutes to let the icing harden.

Jelly beans and gumdrops for decoration.

# A Winter Wonderland

## Who would ever know

that these Christmassy characters in their wintery lands are more than just great-looking faces? Open them and see for yourself.

Hats off to penguins with presents!

# Keep your head or you'll give away the secret!

## Goodies Galore

Don't just build one snowman, make a whole family to guard the presents and keep extra presents safely inside. Create a forest of trees in a snowy land, filled to the brim with gifts and goodies.

The penguin and snowman chat happily, keeping their secrets under their hats!

# HOW TO MAKE GIFT BOXES

**Collect all sorts of tubes,** big or small from potato chip canisters and cookie containers to toilet paper and paper towel rolls – all are perfect for your character boxes. The important thing is to fill them with candy, or other little gifts, and surprise someone on Christmas day.

## Penguin Box

A large tube is perfect for making a performing penguin. When you have mastered the tricky parts, why not try making some smaller penguin chicks?

Measure a good sized beak to stick onto the head.

Glue the band into place.

Cut off a third of the way down the tube.

Cut out two wings from a piece of cardboard.

Wing.

Make a cardboard band and wrap it neatly inside the top part. This will keep the lid on.

Cut out a penguin tail and two flappy feet.

Tape the features to the tube.

## Festive Firs

Hang these trees up by their ribbons or sit them in a foresty lineup. Why not put them around the base of a Christmas tree?

Snip away to make a decorative edge.

When it is dry, curl it into a cone and glue in place.

Paint on some glue patterns and sprinkle them with glitter.

Fold a piece of ribbon in half and cut it so it is twice as long as the cone.

Cut a semicircle of paper to make a cone big enough for your container.

Thread on a bead and push it to the middle.

## Penguin Suit

Cut out a triangle of material.

Put glue along the edge.

Make this edge long enough to fit around the top of the head with a 1/4 in (5 mm) overlap.

Try it on your penguin and trim it until it fits. Glue the sides together.

Glue the hat to the tube.

Add a band and a pompom.

Give him some eyes.

Make clothes out of scraps of material.

Paint the penguin with acrylic paint and craft glue mixed together.

Paint the features using different colors.

*Now fill up your penguin!*

## Dressing the Snowman

Prepare a tube in the same way as the penguin box.

Tape on pipe cleaner arms.

Spread glue on the box and cover it with tufts of cotton balls.

Put a ribbon through the lid and tape it in place.

Try making a junior snowman with a small tube.

Decorate him with material scraps.

Cover a container with wrapping paper for the trunk of the tree.

Make a small hole in the top and thread the ribbon through it.

Pierce two holes in the container and tie the two ribbon ends through them.

Snap on the lid to keep the goodies locked up.

## A forest of firs . . .

. . . filled with fancies

33

# Host of Angels

**Heavenly cookies** adorn the table during the Christmas feast and angelic paper plates flutter gracefully around the sparkling Christmas tree.

## Angel Food

9 oz (250 g) plain flour
4$^1$/$_2$ oz (125 g) butter
2 oz (60 g) sugar

Put all of the ingredients into a bowl and mix them together with your fingers to make crumbs. Slowly knead together to make a ball.

Cook for 10-15 mins
320°F (160°C)

Crush hard candies and put them into the center before you cook them, for a stained glass look.

Roll out the pastry to about $^1$/$_2$ in (1 cm) thick.

Cut a template out of cardboard and use it to cut out the shapes.

Cut a hole in the center of the angels.

Use toothpicks to make patterns.

Silver sugar balls are great for extra decoration.

Cut out shape

Staple the skirt

Decorate the angel

# Flying Angels

A host of cherubs and angels float
dreamily through the sky on
Christmas night. Attach
a piece of string to the
paper angels so that you can
hang them up on branches. Let
the heavenly cookies cool and
delight your family with
your celestial snacks.

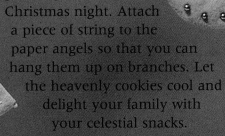

# Santa's Cookie Factory

**Ho, ho, ho,** Santa's been busy rustling up some tasty truffles to tickle the tastebuds.

## Rudolf's Truffles

4¹/₂ oz (125 g) melted butter
9 oz (250 g) crushed graham crackers
4 tablespoons coconut
4 tablespoons cocoa
4 tablespoons honey

*Mix all the ingredients together in the pan*

*Crush the cookies in a bag*

Yum Yum

**Ask an adult . . .**
to melt the butter

## Easy as 1-2-3

The best thing about the truffles is that once the butter has melted there's no more cooking. Ask an adult to melt the butter while you crush the cookies. Let the pan cool before you add the rest of the ingredients.

**Wash your hands . . . .**
before you touch the mixture

*Pour the mixture into a tray*

Divide the mixture into squares with a knife.

Place the tray into the refrigeration for a few hours.

*Roll the squares into balls*

# Magic Marzipan

To make truffle Santas, mix some drops of food coloring into some marzipan, and shape into Santa's features. Try marzipan holly leaves and berries as well for extra plate decoration.

squeeze, roll, and shape into Santa's features

Cover your truffles with delicious decorations

Coconut, chopped nuts, cocoa, or grated chocolate – anything you can think of!

Roll the truffles and place them in paper baking cups.

37

# Frosty Welcomes

**Light up the night** before Christmas with shining ice decorations or glistening ice-bowl lanterns.

## They're illuminating!

Make your garden glow
with Christmassy candlelight

39

# HOW DOES YOUR GARDEN GLOW?

All you need for a Christmas glow is some seasonal cuttings, candles, and lots of ice. You can use anything wintery for your foliage, from holly and ivy to berries and cranberries – just get outside, get picking, and create a welcoming light outside in your garden.

## ⭐ The Big Freeze

Position a small bowl inside a larger one and tape it so that it is hanging in the center – not touching the bottom or sides. Fill the larger bowl with foliage and water, and freeze it.

If the small bowl bobs up too much put some pebbles in it to weigh it down.

## ⭐ Defrost Tip

To remove the bowls, you may have to dip the frozen lantern in warm water, and pour a little into the smaller bowl as well, to loosen the ice

## ⭐ Ice Light

Use half a plastic bottle and a cup for the long lanterns, making sure that the cup doesn't touch the edges of the bottle at all. Use small or tall candles for the inside and if it starts to defrost, perk it up by putting it back into the freezer for a while.

## Ask an adult . . . .

⭐ to light the candles

*Tape the containers*

*Drop in the plants*

Tape the string to the sides of the lid to stop it from moving while it freezes.

## ✦ Ice Art

Find a lid or a tray with at least a 1/2 in (1 cm) tall rim and fill it with water. Put your plant decorations into it then drape the ends of a long piece of string in either side – they will freeze with the ice and can be used to hang it up.

Fill up with water

4
Freeze it all up

5
Let it glow

Find a box your size

and ask an adult . . .

to cut three holes in it
for your arms and head

# Pass the Present

Do you have a
Christmas hat?
If so, put it on!

Decorate a
headband with
tinsel for an
extra sparkle.

If you can fit your
whole body into the
box, it makes a very
cunning disguise.

Complete off
your outfit
by carrying
another package
– you could fill
it with candy.

42

# All you need is a cardboard box to create a present party-piece to parade around in!

## ⭐ Wrap it Up

When you have your arm and head holes, simply wrap up the box using a roll of wrapping paper and adhesive tape.

## ⭐ Ribbons and Bows

To make ribbons and bows, cut long strips of paper and tape them around the box. Fold some extra strips into bow shapes and tape into position.

If you find a big enough box, keep your head inside and make a peephole at the front.

Why not wear a red Christmas outfit underneath your box?

43

# That's Entertainment!

**Family and friends** like nothing more than to sit back, relax, and be entertained. So spoil them with a spectacular show.

## You're a Star ⭐ Abracadabra!

### ✨ Hey Presto!

Know any magic tricks? If so, then create a magician's costume and astonish your audience. If not, then tell a few jokes or a made-up story.

## I'll sing you a song

### ✨ A Bit of a Song and Dance

Sing a few old favorites and encourage the audience to join in, or try your hand at one of the latest songs in the charts. When you have perfected the music, put a dance routine to it.

## Carol Singers

There's nothing better at Christmas than a sing-along of the carols that everyone knows. Perform them at home or persuade an adult to take you out on a tour of the neighborhood. You could collect money for a charity of your choice.

## Hark the Herald Angels Sing . . .

# What a Performance!

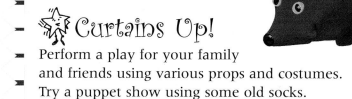

## ⭐ Curtains Up!

Perform a play for your family
and friends using various props and costumes.
Try a puppet show using some old socks.

## A round of applause for . . .

## ⭐ That's Show Business!

Making costumes is easier than you think, all you have
to do is search around your house for odds and ends and
use your imagination. You can create a costume horse
with a rug and a cardboard box, or a fairy with a ballet
outfit and a few homemade props. Invent your own story
or simply use an old favorite.

## Hocus pocus, turn into a horse!

# Welcome to the Christmas Quiz

Try hosting a game show for
your family. Invent your
own game rules and give
away prizes – tempt the
contestants with them at the
beginning of the show.
Invent your own questions
or simply ask them to race
each other with simple tasks.

## Take your seats please

The Christmas Show

Performed by:
The Festive players

Act One: Aunty Jill arrives
Act Two: Disaster Dessert
Interval
Act Three: Jamie saves the day!
Grand Finale

Draw your own program for a
show. Why not pretend to be
members of your family and
act out a family scene. Be
careful not to upset anyone!

# Packing Presents

**It's the night** before Christmas and as dusk falls stockings are waiting to be filled through the night. So surprise Santa with these bright ones!

Attach a loop at the top so that you can hang it up.

Stick all of the decorations on with a fabric glue. It will say on the tube if it is suitable.

Cut out two sock shapes and stick them together with a fabric glue.

Make them big — Santa's stuffing more in this year!

Cut Rudolph's face shape out of felt and stick it to the stocking. Use different colors for the features.

## ⭐ A Stitch in Time

To jazz up the stocking, try your hand at blanket stitch around the edges.

Start the stitch by putting the needle through about 1/2 in (1 cm) away from the edge.

Bring the thread under the needle as you pull it down and through — it's as simple as that!

## ✦ Stick 'em Up!

If the stockings are ready then it's almost Christmas day. Hurray! Hang it up to wait for Santa, or you could make one as a gift for someone special.

These felt snowflakes prove that you don't have to use a lot of colors to get a great Christmas look.

The best thing about these stockings is that you can use them year after year.

# INDEX

Advent calendar 4-8
Angel 18, 21, 34, 35

Bauble 14-17, 18, 22
Bell 11, 28
Box 4, 5, 6, 7, 32, 42, 43, 45

Candle 38, 40
Candy cane 29
Candy cup 21
Card 8, 10, 11, 15, 16, 21, 32
Carol singers 44
Chalet 28, 29
Christmas day 32, 47
Christmas eve 6
Christmas quiz 45
Christmas show 45
Christmas tree 10, 18-21, 32, 34
Cookie factory 28, 36-37
Costume 42-43, 44, 45

Decorations 18-21, 34, 37, 38, 41

Entertainment 44-45

Fold-out card 10-11
Frosty 22, 23, 38

Gift Box 30-33
Glitter 18, 21, 22, 26, 27, 32
Glycerine 26, 27
Greeting card 8-11

Heavenly biscuit 34, 35

Ice decoration 38-42
Ice lantern 38-41

Jar 24, 26, 27

Magician 44
Marzipan 37
Merry mobiles 22-23

Orbs 14-17

Packing presents 46-47
Paper doily 29
Paper plate 16, 17, 34

Paper snow 12-13
Parcel 8, 10, 11, 42, 43
Pass the Present 42-43
Penguin 25, 30, 31, 32, 33
Table-tennis Ball 18, 21, 22
Pompom 14-17
Pop-up card 11
Puppet show 45

Reindeer 29
Ribbon 21, 27, 32, 33, 43
Rudolph 9, 11, 22, 23, 36, 46

Salt dough 20
Santa 9, 11, 18, 20, 22, 28, 29, 36, 37, 46, 47
Sleigh 28, 29

Snow 24, 29, 31
Snowflake 12, 47
Snowman 9, 10, 11, 22, 31, 33
Snowstorm 12, 24-27
Star 6, 7, 9, 11, 18, 21, 25
Stocking 46, 47

Tinsel 7, 42
Tree 10, 12, 14, 16, 18, 19, 21, 22, 31, 32, 33
Truffle 36, 37

Winter Wonderland 26, 30-31
Wrapping paper 15, 16, 33, 43

# ACKNOWLEDGEMENTS

With additional thanks to . . .
Maisie Armah, Charlotte Bull, Billy Bull, James Bull,
Sorcha Lyons, and Kailen Wilcox for being merry models.
Additional photography:
Dave King for the magician page 44, the fairy and the pantomime horse page 45
Steve Shott for the carol singers page 39, 44